Harp Seals

Animals of the Snow and Ice

Elaine Landau

Contents

Words to Know

blubber—The layer of fat under the skin of an animal.

global warming—A rise in Earth's temperature. This warming causes climate change.

hakapik—A club used by hunters to kill seals.

herd—A large group of animals.

molt—To lose an outer covering of fur or feathers so that a new covering can grow.

prey—An animal that is hunted by another animal for food.

A baby harp seal is at home in the snow and ice.

An Animal of the Sea, Snow, and Ice

It is early April, but you feel cold. You know the reason why. You have come up to the North Atlantic Ocean to study animals.

At first all you see are snow-covered ice floes. Ice floes are large pieces of floating ice in the sea. Then you take a closer look. What you thought were clumps of snow are really baby animals.

They have fluffy white fur, big dark eyes, and flippers. They are cute enough to be stuffed toys. Yet they are very much alive.

You have come across a group of two-week-old harp seal pups. They are at home in an icy, cold place. They are animals of the sea, snow, and ice.

Adult harp seals have U-shaped marks on their backs that look like harps.

What a Seal!

It is hard to miss an adult harp seal. These sleek animals have large blimp-shaped bodies. Males can grow to over six feet long. That is about a foot longer than most bathtubs.

Male harp seals can weigh close to 300 pounds. Imagine picking up three twelve-year-old children at once. That is what it would be like to pick up a male harp seal. Females are a little smaller.

Adult harp seals have black heads and silver-gray bodies. They also have large U-shaped markings on their backs. The marks look like harps. That is why they are called harp seals.

Harp seals hear quite well. Yet they don't have ears on the outside of their heads like we do. They have two small ear openings instead. This helps them glide more smoothly through the water. Sometimes harp seals are called earless seals. Seals with ears on the outside are called sea lions.

Getting Around

Harp seals are fast, graceful swimmers. They have flippers instead of feet. Their powerful back flippers move from side to side. This sends them speedily through the water. Harp seals can reach speeds of up to 15 miles per hour. That is about three times faster than the fastest human swimmers.

Harp seals use their front flippers for steering. These flippers have sharp claws. Their claws help the seals climb onto ice floes. They grasp the ice like hooks.

Harp seals move faster in the water than on the ice. Their back limbs cannot be turned forward. That means they have to wriggle and pull their bodies along the ice. Some people think they move like giant caterpillars.

Harp seals are built for swimming. They are not as good at moving on the land.

Home Sweet Home

Harp seals live in the area that is colored orange on this map.

Harp seals are at home in the cold, icy sea. These animals live off the coasts of Norway, Russia, Greenland, and Canada. They also live in the Gulf of St. Lawrence. They swim in the freezing waters of the North Atlantic and Arctic Oceans. The waters they live in are largely covered with sea ice and snow.

Harp seals escape some of the coldest weather, though. They travel south for the winter. They return home in the summer. Some swim as far as 3,000 miles to do this.

Harp seals are very social animals. They live together in groups called herds. They travel in herds as well. Groups of them can be spotted swimming together.

Harp seals like to live
together in groups.

Suited for the Sea, Snow, and Ice

Harp seals are built to swim. They are also great divers. They can reach a depth of about 600 feet. They can hold their breath a long time. During a dive, harp seals can stay underwater for thirty minutes!

You might think that a cold, snowy piece of ice is not a very nice place to live. But these seals do not mind the cold. In fact, their scientific name means "ice loving." They have a thick layer of **blubber** beneath their skin. This helps them keep the cold out and their body heat in.

Harp seals can hold their breath for a long time, so they are great divers.

Harp seal pups blend in easily
with the snow.

Young seal pups fit in well with their new home. The pups' fur coats are clear. They look white and blend in with the snow. Their enemies cannot easily see them. But the seals can see their enemies a long way off on the ice.

Time to Dine

Harp seals are big eaters. They have to eat a lot. They need to keep their thick layer of blubber. A skinny seal would not last long in the cold.

These animals are meat eaters. Living in the sea, they eat lots of different fish. Among these are cod, halibut, herring, and redfish. They also eat shellfish such as shrimp, prawns, and crabs.

Harp seals do not chew their food. They swallow small fish whole. They use their pointed teeth to tear off chunks of larger prey. They swallow these pieces whole too. When they eat fish, they sometimes take a bite out of the belly and leave the rest.

Larger animals feed on harp seals. Sharks, orcas, and polar bears hunt them. A polar bear can smell a seal twenty miles away.

Harp seals like to eat crabs, redfish, and shrimp.

Crab

Redfish

Shrimp

Mating Season

Harp seals mate when they go south for the winter. The males chase the females on the ice. They have special mating calls. Sometimes, a male will fight another male for a female. Beneath the water, the males blow bubbles at the females. Mating takes place underwater as well as on the ice.

These three male seals
are waiting for females.

About a year later, the females give birth. Large numbers of females come together to have their babies on the floating ice. Each usually has just one baby, called a pup. The baby seals are born between late February and early March. In about two weeks, their mothers will be ready to mate again.

Harp seals usually have
only one pup.

Here Come the Pups

Newborn harp seals are cute but helpless. These young pups cannot swim or feed themselves. They need their mothers for everything.

Groups of female harp seals nurse their young on ice floes at sea. The mother's milk is very rich and almost as thick as wax. The pups gain weight very quickly. Soon they have their own layer of blubber to keep them warm.

The females spend only a short time on the ice with their young. After about twelve days they are ready to go back to the sea. Soon they will begin their journey north.

The pups are left alone on the ice. They live off their body fat. When they are three weeks old, they molt and lose their fluffy white fur. They no longer look like powder puffs. They grow new thicker coats that are better suited to the water.

When they are about twenty-five days old, the young seals are able to swim. They can find food for themselves as well. Now they can go to sea to begin the long trip north.

When harp seal pups are three weeks old, they start to lose their white fur and grow new, adult fur.

Harp seals are in danger from global warming and hunters.

Hard Times for Harp Seals

Some herds of harp seals are in trouble. This is partly due to global warming. As the climate gets warmer, the sea ice melts. That leaves fewer places where seals can mate and have their young. They have to swim farther to find suitable areas.

Humans have hunted seals for hundreds of years. Older harp seals are hunted for their oil, fur, and skin. Their oil has lots of vitamins. The fur and skin are used to make clothing. Meat from seal flippers is sometimes used in meat pies.

Seals are usually hunted with rifles. Sometimes they are hunted with a club called a hakapik. The seals suffer if they are not killed quickly.

These people will give the
baby seal a health exam.

Save Those Seals!

Many people are trying to help the harp seal and other Arctic animals. They are working with businesses and governments to find ways to lessen global warming. This will reduce the loss of sea ice.

People have also tried to stop the seal hunts. They have made the public aware that these animals are sometimes killed in a cruel way. Countries have taken action too.

Canada has limited the times seals can be hunted and the number that can be killed. It has also put limits on the ways that these animals can be killed. The United States and some countries in Europe do not buy things made from harp seals.

Yet harp seals remain in danger. The effects of global warming still put them at risk. Hunters continue to kill them. More seals die every year. We must do all we can to help them. Harp seals have a right to their place in the world.

Fun Facts About Harp Seals

- Harp seals are also called saddleback seals. The marking on their backs looks like a saddle.

- Fossil remains of harp seals date back 20 million years.

- Harp seals can live for 35 years or more.

- Harp seals can sense the water's temperature through their whiskers. These hairs act like feelers.

- Harp seal mothers know their young. They can pick their pup out of a large group by its scent.

- Because of the rich harp seal milk, harp seal pups grow very fast. At less than two weeks old, a baby seal can weigh as much as 80 pounds.

Learn More

Books

Mack, Laurie. *Arctic and Antarctic*. New York: DK Publishing, Inc., 2006.

Martin-James, Kathleen. *Harp Seals*. Minneapolis, Minn.: Lerner Publishing Group, 2009.

Townsend, Emily Rose. *Seals*. Mankato, Minn.: Capstone Press, 2006.

Twine, Alice. *Seals*. New York: Rosen Publishing Group, 2007.

Web Sites

Kids 4 Seals

http://www.kids4seals.org/

Harp Seals

http://animals.national geographic.com/animals/ mammals/harp-seal.html

Index

Enslow Elementary, an imprint of Enslow Publishers, Inc.
Enslow Elementary® is a registered trademark of Enslow Publishers, Inc.

Library of Congress Cataloging-in-Publication Data

Landau, Elaine.
  Harp seals : animals of the snow and ice / by Elaine Landau.
      p. cm. — (Animals of the snow and ice)
  Includes bibliographical references and index.
  Summary: "Provides information for young readers about harp seals, including habitat, eating habits, mating, babies, and conservation"—Provided by publisher.
  ISBN 978-0-7660-3460-0
  1. Harp seal—Juvenile literature. I. Title.
  QL737.P64L36 2011
  599.79'29—dc22
                                    2009006480

Printed in the United States of America

112009 Lake Book Manufacturing, Inc., Melrose Park, IL

10 9 8 7 6 5 4 3 2 1

To Our Readers: We have done our best to make sure all Internet Addresses in this book were active and appropriate when we went to press. However, the author and the publisher have no control over and assume no liability for the material available on those Internet sites or on other Web sites they may link to. Any comments or suggestions can be sent by e-mail to comments@enslow.com or to the address on the back cover.

♻ Enslow Publishers, Inc., is committed to printing our books on recycled paper. The paper in every book contains 10% to 30% post-consumer waste (PCW). The cover board on the outside of each book contains 100% PCW. Our goal is to do our part to help young people and the environment too!

Photo Credits: © All Canada Photos/photolibrary, p. 6; © 1999, Artville, LLC, p. 10; © Biosphoto/Bruemmer Fred/Peter Arnold Inc., p. 11; © Biosphoto/Cordier Sylvain/Peter Arnold Inc., p. 24; © ChoiceGraphX/iStockphoto.com, p. 17 (redfish); Discovery Channel Images/Getty Images, pp. 2–3; © Doug Allan/naturepl.com, p. 23; © Gerard Lacz/Animals Animals, p. 4; © JoLin/iStockphoto.com, p. 17 (shrimp); © Juniors Bildarchiv/photolibrary, p. 29; © 2009 Jupiterimages Corporation, a Getty Images Company, p. 30; © M. Watson/ardea.com, p. 26; © McDonald Wildlife Photog./Animals Animals, p. 19; © Michio Hoshino/Minden Pictures, p. 9; © Vebjørn Karlsen/iStockphoto.com, p. 17 (crab); ©Mitsuaki Iwago/Minden Pictures, p. 14; National Geographic/Getty Images, p. 13; REUTERS/Paul Darrow/Landov, p. 1; Shutterstock, pp. 20–21, 32.

Cover Photo: REUTERS/Paul Darrow/Landov

Enslow Elementary
an imprint of
Enslow Publishers, Inc.
40 Industrial Road
Box 398
Berkeley Heights, NJ 07922
USA
http://www.enslow.com